D0097523

one

This book is provided for your reading pleasure and inspiration. May you experience God's blessings as you read it. Please take the book home and after you have read it, pass it on to someone else. God bless you!

ATTACH 2.5" X 2.5"

PHOTO OF

YOU & YOUR SPOUSE.

Date

One Devotional

MarriageToday™
PO Box 59888
Dallas, Texas 75229

1-800-380-6330

marriagetoday.com

Unless otherwise noted, all Scripture references and quotations
are taken from the New King James Version (NKJV), copyright
1979, 1980, 1982, Thomas Nelson, Inc. Publishers.

ISBN 978-1-931585-23-7

10 9 8 7 6 5 4 3 2

Printed in the United States of America

Table of Contents

Introduction

Foundations
Applying a few basic principles

Relationship
Creating a culture of love

Connection
Learning and growing together

Imagination
Desiring the best for your marriage

Experience
Loving the couple you are becoming

Appendix

Introduction

You may have heard the story about the two people who met in an online chat room and began an Internet romance. From the start, they were amazed at how much they had in common. They found each other to be kind and compassionate, and they even shared the fact that they were both trapped in miserable marriages with spouses who were cold and insensitive.

This man and woman arranged to meet, and in the process they made a shocking discovery: They were married to each other! That's right, this couple fell in love on the Internet while living under the same roof in an unfulfilled and loveless marriage.

This story is simultaneously funny and sad. It also drives home the point that true happiness is often closer than you think it is. The person you fell in love with and married is your best hope for a happy, mutually satisfying marriage. All it takes is a commitment to make your marriage the best it can be, and that's the purpose of the devotional book you hold in your hands.

Over the next 52 weeks, you will wisely invest time and energy into building the marriage of your dreams. The year is divided into five sections, and the topics include everything from communication and finances to romance and vision for the future, just to name a few. As the weeks progress, you will learn more about each other and yourselves. I truly believe that as you focus your attention on improving your marriage, you will notice your relationship changing and your love for each other growing deeper.

Each week's devotional has four parts. First is a Scripture that corresponds with that week's theme. I recommend that you commit the verse to memory and spend time meditating on it throughout the week. Next is the weekly devotional, which you will read together. That's followed by thought-provoking questions and ideas for you to discuss and apply to your life. Finally, there are action steps to take, which may include a fun activity or a specific way to express your love to each other.

To get started, the first step is to choose a day and time that fits your schedule. The best advice I can give you is this: have fun and enjoy spending this time together! Each week as you invest quality time in your relationship, your new and improved marriage will begin to take shape. May God richly bless you as you commit to building a marriage that will last a lifetime.

Foundations

Applying a few basic principles

Week 1

A Blessed Marriage

God created man in His own image; in the image of God He created him; male and female He created them. Then God blessed them. (Genesis 1:27-28)

If you could ask God to do anything for you—what would it be?

It's my hope that one of the first things you would think to ask Him to do would be to bless your marriage. After all, in God's heart, marriage is a priority. We know that because of this passage from the Book of Genesis.

Here we find that God created man and woman, and then He *immediately* established marriage. Marriage was God's idea, and He blessed Adam and Eve's. Verse 31 tells us: "God saw everything that He had made, and indeed it was *very good.*" Adam and Eve's marriage was very good as a result of God's blessing—they had the perfect marriage!

The word *blessed* in this passage of scripture means "*to endue with power for success, prosperity, fertility and longevity.*" When God blessed them, His Spirit came upon Adam and Eve and empowered them to succeed in every area. God was an active participant in their lives. As long as they followed His will for their marriage, they experienced great blessing. Their marriage was *very good*!

However when Adam and Eve rejected God's involvement and made decisions solo, they moved out from under His blessing and experienced the curse instead. The same thing happens in marriages today—some marriages are wonderfully blessed while others are miserable. This isn't because God has favorites. It's due to the fact that some couples are following God's will, while others aren't. Really, it's a choice.

When you yield your life and marriage to God's will, you can expect Him to bless it. That's also when you begin to experience a little bit of heaven on earth!

Talk It Out 💬
Spend a few minutes identifying the areas of your marriage in which you are experiencing God's blessing. Are there other areas that might be lacking in blessing because you haven't asked for God's involvement or sought His will in the decisions you've made? These areas might include finances, communication, your friendships, sensitivity to each other's needs, etc. Take a few minutes to pray together and recommit every area of your marriage to God.

Walk It Out ☑
Make a special gesture to your spouse this week that tells what a blessing he or she is in your life.

Write It Out 📓

His

_____

_____

_____

_____

_____

_____

_____

Hers

_____

_____

_____

_____

_____

_____

_____

Week 2

Your Deepest Need

Whoever drinks of this water will thirst again, but whoever drinks of the water that I shall give him will never thirst. But the water that I shall give him will become in him a fountain of water springing up into everlasting life. (John 4:13-14)

In the fourth chapter of John's gospel, Jesus ministered to a Samaritan woman who had been married five times and was currently living together with a man. She was at a well near her hometown, drawing water. She was there by herself, a clear indication that she was an outcast in her community—other women avoided associating with her.

But Jesus loved her. He didn't approve of her lifestyle—but He valued her as a person. He also knew the root cause of her marriage problems and was there to help her solve her chronic issue with men. The problem was that she was looking for men to meet needs within her that only God could meet.

We have four basic human needs that drive all of us at all times. Those needs are acceptance, identity, security, and purpose. Even though we can get these needs met on a human level to a degree, only God can truly meet these needs on the deepest level. This was the water Jesus was referring to that would completely satisfy the inner thirst that men had never been able to quench.

The most important issue in marriage is our personal, daily relationship with Christ. If we will look to Him to meet our deepest needs, we will be satisfied and be able to relate in a healthy way with our spouse and others. However, if we are not in relationship with Jesus in a meaningful way, we will naturally transfer to our spouse the expectation of meeting our needs. The result is that we are set up for disappointment and our spouse is set up for failure.

The best thing you can do for your marriage is to cultivate your relationship with the Lord. Spend time with the Lord every day—praying, reading your Bible, and asking for God's help in everyday decisions in your life. Also take time regularly to pray together over important issues. Practicing these simple principles will go a long way in building a solid foundation for your marriage.

Talk It Out 💬

Share with each other about the time you chose to begin a personal relationship with Christ. Talk about what that relationship means to you today. If you have never made that decision, see the appendix of this book to learn more.

Walk It Out ☑

Designate a time this week to spend a few minutes praying together about issues you are facing as a couple. End by praying a special blessing over each other.

Write It Out 📄
Week 2

His

_____

_____

_____

_____

_____

_____

_____

Hers

_____

_____

_____

_____

_____

_____

_____

A Special Kind of Love

The fruit of the Spirit is love, joy, peace, longsuffering, kindness, goodness, faithfulness, gentleness, self-control. (Galatians 5:22-23)

There is an odd truth concerning love and marriage. Understanding it is an important key in making marriage and other relationships work. The truth is this: we don't have the ability to really love without the power of the Holy Spirit working through us. Our capacity to love is based on God giving us that ability, supernaturally, as we surrender to Him.

So how are people able to "love" when they don't know God? They can't. At least they are not able to love with God's type of love. God's love is a special love the Bible calls *agape*. It is a love that flows out of the will and does not change. It is the most stable and predictable kind of love and the only type that can provide a lasting foundation in marriage.

Often, when people say they love someone, they are just talking about sexual desire (the Greek word *eros*, from which we get the word *erotic*) or a passionate feeling (*thumos*, from which we get our *thermos*). These kinds of feelings come and go. When they go for very long, many people give the old line, "I don't love you anymore," and they are out the door.

Agape love, however, is a committed and sacrificial love that is modeled after Jesus. When Jesus tells us He loves us, He isn't talking about a feeling that comes and goes. He is telling us He is committed to us forever and will not change. Whether

His feelings for us are positive or negative, it doesn't change His commitment to us.

Consider what you mean when you tell each other, "I love you." Are you saying that you are experiencing a fleeting feeling, or are you saying you are committed to each other forever and will demonstrate love regardless of bad feelings or negative circumstances? It isn't wrong to express a feeling, as long as when that feeling isn't there anymore, you can still say, "I love you," and do the right thing regardless of the situation.

The most stable and dependable people in relationships are those who are submitted to the influence of the Holy Spirit. They are empowered by a supernatural love that will do the right thing through thick and thin. God's agape love is the highest form of love and it will transform any person, relationship, or marriage under its influence.

Talk It Out 💬
Think of a time that you made a choice to do the right thing, even though it was difficult (telling the truth, standing up for another person, etc.). Talk about those experiences and what you learned from them.

Walk It Out ☑
Buy a greeting card to give to your spouse this week. If you both enjoy a good laugh, make it a humorous card. Whether funny or serious, use it as a chance to reaffirm the depth of your commitment to each other.

Write It Out 📋

His

Hers

First Things First

Therefore a man shall leave his father and mother and be joined to his wife, and they shall become one flesh. (Genesis 2:24)

When God created marriage, He had a plan. In order to understand God's plan, we must begin by realizing the importance of priority in our lives. The first thing God ever said in the Bible concerning marriage was that a man would have to leave his father and mother to be joined to a wife. Leaving our father or mother doesn't mean that we can't see them anymore or that they aren't important to us. It simply means that they must be reprioritized in our lives and that our spouse must take the number-one spot—with the exception of our relationship with Christ.

Marriage only works if it is first in our lives. In my book *Marriage on the Rock*, I call this The Law of Priority. God created marriage to operate as the most important human relationship in our lives, and it only succeeds on that level. It is more important than children, work, friends, or anything else except for God Himself.

When marriage is first, it thrives. In fact, it's how you fall in love and stay in love. Because you prioritize the relationship and focus on each other first, there is a great deal of passion and good will in the relationship.

Priority means you give each other the first and best of your time, energy, and focus. Lack of priority means you are transferring your best to someone or something else. In marriage, this creates legitimate jealousy and problems. Whether it is a husband who is distracted by work or a wife who is too absorbed in the kids—it is going to cause trouble. By the way, most things that violate the law of priority are actually good and necessary things—like work or children. The problem is they should never take priority over the marriage.

Priority must be proven daily in real terms and not just in words. Good intentions mean very little in marriage. The only thing that matters is what you do and continue to do consistently. For your marriage to work, you must establish it as the first priority and be willing to protect it against good or bad things that try to distract you.

Talk It Out 💬
If you recognize that you have made mistakes in this area, apologize and ask your spouse to forgive you. Talk about ways you can rearrange your individual schedules and priorities to protect your time and energy for each other.

Walk It Out ☑
Take a break from your usual responsibilities at least once this week and take a walk together or go out for coffee or dessert. Make it a time to let your spouse know your relationship is the most important priority in your life.

Write It Out

His

Hers

A Passionate Pursuit

Therefore a man shall leave his father and mother and <u>be joined</u> to his wife. (Genesis 2:24)

This week we are going to talk about the second law of marriage—the Law of Pursuit. I underlined the words *be joined* in the Scripture above because these words are very important in understanding marriage. Even though the words look mundane on the outside—they are dynamic. They literally mean that a man is to "cling" to his wife for a lifetime. It also includes women in their relationships with their husbands.

The Hebrew word for "joined" or "cling" is the word *dabaq*. It is a very energetic word that means "to pursue with great zeal." In the very beginning God told us the truth about marriage—it is work! That's right! Marriage is work, and it only works when you work at it.

Couples fall in love because they work at the relationship. They try hard to impress each other, are careful to be sensitive to each other, and try to please one another. But then, once they are comfortable in the relationship, they start taking each other for granted and change the energetic behaviors that caused them to fall in love in the first place. The result is lost passion, boredom, and tension.

This is exactly what Karen and I did when we first got married. Our relationship began with an enormous amount of passion and goodwill that lasted for years. However, the more comfortable I became with the fact that Karen was going to stay with me, the more I took her for granted and the more I turned my attention to work, friends, and the pursuit of money. The result was constant fighting that left us passionless and on the brink of divorce.

The resurrection of our marriage didn't come through any emotional breakthrough. It came as we realized what caused the breakdown—laziness, apathy, and taking each other for granted. When we realized this, we changed and started working at the relationship. As we did, the feelings slowly returned. Over time, they grew deeper and deeper and they have never stopped.

That was over thirty years ago, and today we have a very passionate marriage—because we work at it. Even after all of these years we know that if we don't keep exerting effort toward each other and keep our marriage first—we will start experiencing problems.

Talk It Out 💬

Do you feel that you sometimes take each other for granted? In what ways? Talk about some practical steps you can take to begin pursuing each other the way you did when you were dating.

Walk It Out ☑

Next time you're in the car together, reach for your spouse's hand. The simple act of holding hands communicates an active interest in pleasing your spouse.

Write It Out 📝

Week 5

His

Hers

It's All in the Sharing

Let the husband render to his wife the affection due her, and likewise also the wife to her husband. The wife does not have authority over her own body, but the husband does. And likewise the husband does not have authority over his own body, but the wife does.
(1 Corinthians 7:3-4)

When God created marriage, He created foundational laws for it to be guided and guarded. One of those laws is the Law of Possession. It is stated in Genesis 2:24: "*They shall become one flesh.*" Once you are married, you are no longer two but one.

Certainly, this relates to the beauty of sexual intimacy that is unique within the marriage relationship. But it also goes far beyond that; in fact, it is a profoundly important concept to understand. The law of possession means that for marriage to work, you must share everything and possess nothing apart from one another.

The words of the Apostle Paul in 1 Corinthians reveal how God created marriage to produce the deepest intimacy and bonding possible in a human relationship. Once a couple is married, each one must yield the rights over his or her own body. This isn't a license for abuse; it is a guarantee of use for both husband and wife to get their needs met.

In God's design, you can't withhold from each other. You must give everything you have to each other and share everything. This is why it is called "the law of possession."

The only way two different individuals can become one is if both are willing to take what was theirs individually and now surrender it to the common cause.

Marriage is about sharing your lives with each other. That requires giving of yourself and caring for each other. It means you don't make decisions without the agreement of your spouse. It means you don't withdraw sex or anything else in the relationship to punish or control. It means all of the money and assets of the family belong to both of you equally, regardless of where they came from or who worked to earn them.

Selfishness and independence destroy the spirit of marriage. Giving and sharing create the strongest bond of intimacy possible. This intimacy is so powerful that the word used to describe it is "one." Two people becoming one heart, one home and one mind as they lay aside their individualism and selfishness—that is what marriage is all about.

Talk It Out 💬
In your marriage, how well are you following the principles of the Law of Possession—surrendering it all and sharing everything equally? Talk about any areas you feel you need to work on. If a more detailed explanation would be helpful, see chapter five of my book *Marriage on the Rock*.

Walk It Out ☑
Find a time to have a special intimate night together. Send the kids to a babysitter's or family member's house, or plan an overnight getaway for just the two of you.

Jimmy Evans

Write It Out 📝
Week 6

His

_____

_____

_____

_____

_____

_____

_____

_____

Hers

_____

_____

_____

_____

_____

_____

_____

_____

Naked and Unashamed

And they were both naked, the man and his wife, and were not ashamed. (Genesis 2:25)

It is interesting that when God created Adam and Eve in the Garden of Eden, He created them naked and without any shame related to it. The word "naked" in Genesis 2:25 means "to be exposed." In other words, God created marriage to be a place where you could totally expose yourselves to each other—*mentally, emotionally, spiritually, sexually, and physically*—without shame.

This is what makes intimacy on every level possible in marriage. When you are truly "naked" without shame in marriage, you can share your lives with each other. You have unhindered access to each other. You can talk about anything without fear. You can express your sexuality without inhibition. You can share your darkest feelings and brightest dreams with each other without a thought of future reproach.

All of this is true under one condition—that the relationship remains pure. You see, when Adam and Eve were created, they were naked without shame until sin entered into the relationship. Once they sinned, they could no longer trust each other. Paradise was lost as they both retreated under fig leaves and shivered in fear, separated from intimacy with God and each other.

The good news is this—couples can find their way back to paradise. It begins as you take responsibility for your actions and apologize for any damaging behavior. As you both do this, you will create an atmosphere of purity in your relationship—the fig leaves will be removed and your intimacy will return.

To keep the purity in your relationship, you must be careful in how you treat each other. You also must monitor your words, attitudes, and actions to make sure you don't become sloppy and take each other for granted. When you make a mistake, apologize quickly. This is the only way to create a "naked" marriage the way God intended.

Talk It Out 🗩

In what areas of your marriage are you reluctant to let down your guard and become "naked" before each other (mentally, emotionally, spiritually, sexually, physically)? Talk about mistakes you have made and positive changes you can make to improve your level of intimacy.

Walk It Out ☑

Tell each other about a specific dream you have for the future. Take the initial steps toward letting yourself be vulnerable, and be sure to affirm each other and let each other know that your marriage is a safe place to be open and honest.

Write It Out 📄

His

_____

_____

_____

_____

_____

_____

_____

Hers

_____

_____

_____

_____

_____

_____

_____

Week 8

Talk it Up

A man has joy by the answer of his mouth, and a word spoken in due season, how good it is! (Proverbs 15:23)

Communication is a huge issue in marriage. It is the first point of contact when you initially meet, and it provides the foundation for relational growth. Because it is so important as a foundation, there are some things to remember.

First of all, a wise master builder never overbuilds on a foundation. You simply cannot establish a superstructure on a foundation that is either too small, too thin, or too weak. Likewise, your marriage cannot grow beyond the foundation of communication.

Regardless of how long you've been married, communication can never become a secondary issue. In other words, sex, money, children, houses, or any aspect of marriage cannot take the place of communication as the primary base of your marriage.

When you have a house with foundation problems, the problems are typically more visible in other areas than with the foundation. Cracks in the walls, doors that won't close, and loose flooring are merely symptoms of the real problem. You can patch and fix all you want, but you're just going to have to keep doing it over and over again until you fix the foundation.

It is the same in marriage. When you have communication problems, it shows up in every other area. For example, when you're not communicating you begin fighting about money, the kids, and other things. Also, it has a significant impact on your sex life. This is especially true for women.

Communication takes time and energy. Regardless of how busy you are or what sacrifices you have to make, take time to talk. Many years ago when this was a big issue for Karen and me, we took time after we put the kids to bed to sit face-to-face and talk. It transformed our marriage on every level.

We have never stopped. We talk a lot every day and we love it. It is the basis for everything we do in our marriage. It really never gets more complicated than that.

If you've become lazy in communicating, get to work and realize the importance of this issue. The more you learn to communicate, the stronger your marriage will be and the higher it can go.

Talk It Out 💬
Sit in a comfortable chair or on the couch, facing each other, and take turns talking and listening. Do this for at least ten to fifteen minutes. It may seem uncomfortable at first, but as you relax and begin to enjoy it, you'll discover you really do have interesting things to talk about!

Walk It Out ☑
Turn off the television, put down the newspaper or magazine, and take a walk together one evening. Talk about the events of your day and reconnect with each other.

Jimmy Evans

Write It Out 📄

His

_____

_____

_____

_____

_____

_____

_____

_____

Hers

_____

_____

_____

_____

_____

_____

_____

_____

Gentle Truth

A gentle answer turns away wrath, but a harsh word stirs up anger. (Proverbs 15:1, NIV)

One time Karen and I were having a fight. I remember how frustrated I was. I kept trying to tell her how I felt and convince her that she was wrong. I wasn't making any progress, which only made me more frustrated. At one point in the conversation, I remember Karen saying to me, "Jimmy, I wish I had an audio recording of how you talk to me. You wouldn't believe how harsh you are." I immediately reacted to what she said. "I'm not harsh with you!" I insisted (with my voice raised).

Several days later I was praying about what Karen had said. I was reading in Ephesians where it says that Jesus washes His Bride *"with the washing of water by the word"* (Ephesians 5:26). Immediately, in my mind, I saw myself standing before Jesus, filthy in my sins. The next thing I saw was Jesus filling His hands with water and very gently pouring it over my head. He wasn't at all harsh with the application of His Word. Just the opposite, He was so gentle and loving.

The next thing the Lord showed me troubled me greatly. I saw Karen standing in front of me in a beautiful wedding gown. The gown had some stains on it and I was washing her down with a fire hose. The force of the fire hose was causing Karen pain and tearing her beautiful gown apart.

At once I knew that the Lord was showing me the difference between His nature and mine when it came to communication and trying to change others. I repented to God in that moment and changed my ways immediately.

The next time I confronted Karen, I decided to speak in a loving manner and leave the results to God. It wasn't long before she noticed the difference in me. As soon as I changed, Karen began to blossom like a rose. Our relationship became so much better.

Now, I can say how I feel and leave the outcome to God. I have found that He is much better at changing people and producing results than I am. Sometimes I am the one who needs to change, and God is always faithful to reveal that to me in His loving and kind way.

Tell each other the truth, but do it in love and don't try to be the enforcer. Remember, the truth is powerful. It doesn't need our help. Just lovingly apply it, and it will do wonders!

Talk It Out 💬
How do you communicate with each other when you are frustrated about something? Talk about ways to improve your approach—tone of voice, body language, choice of words, etc.

Walk It Out ☑
Choose gentle words to speak to your spouse, and see how he or she blossoms with your praise.

Write It Out 📝

His

Hers

A Little Care Repair

Kind words are like honey—sweet to the soul and healthy for the body. (Proverbs 16:24, NLT)

Every couple faces communication challenges in their marriage. I've faced my own challenges, taught on the subject for many years, and learned there is one element necessary for success—caring.

That's right. It doesn't matter what communication techniques you may know and understand—if you don't care, it won't make a difference.

The actual breakdown of communication in marriage typically begins when attitudes begin to change. For instance, when you first began dating, you had long conversations about your lives, future, expectations, etc. And things were great! Why? Because you cared! You worked to understand each other and affirm the importance of what the other person had to say. This is one reason you fell in love and became willing to commit in a deeper way to the relationship.

Fast forward into the marriage when communication begins to break down and you'll find a different story. The lack of face-to-face, meaningful time together combined with sarcastic retorts, eye rolling, negative facial gestures and just a basic lack of caring about what your spouse is feeling or saying will devastate the atmosphere of positive communication.

For your marriage to be successful, you're going to have to have an open line of communication. For that to happen, you both need to feel safe enough to share your thoughts and feelings with each other. That will only take place if you feel as though the other person really cares.

Caring is communicated by eye contact, a positive countenance, providing positive feedback as your spouse shares, valuing his or her input, and simply doing anything you can to let them know you care. Also, as you care about your partner, it will become easier to understand the opposite sex. It's really not that hard to figure out the person you are married to if you really care about him or her. However, if you don't have personal concern for each other, your marriage can quickly become a dark mystery with danger at every turn.

Ready to try a little "care repair" in your marriage? It will go a long way toward getting the communication in your marriage back on track. When that happens, you'll automatically experience a rise in the romantic temperature of your relationship! As long as you keep communicating how much you care, the temperature of romance will continue to increase.

Talk It Out 🗩
Have you communicated lately how much you care about each other? Are you experiencing a breakdown in communication because of some of the negative traits listed above? If so, talk about ways to make positive changes in these areas.

Walk It Out ☑
Show your spouse how much you care by making eye contact and giving positive feedback during your next conversation.

Jimmy Evans

Write It Out 📝
Week 10

His

_____

_____

_____

_____

_____

_____

_____

Hers

_____

_____

_____

_____

_____

_____

_____

The Power of Words

Death and life are in the power of the tongue, and those who love it will eat its fruit. (Proverbs 18:21)

Communication in marriage is a lifeline of information, conflict resolution and affection. To be able to communicate effectively, you must understand the disproportionate power of words.

In relationships, words are tremendously powerful for good or bad. In every good relationship, there is an exchange of many positive words. These words act as seeds that create a powerful and disproportionate harvest. The same is true in bad relationships. In every bitter or unsatisfactory marriage, there are either few words exchanged (few seeds planted) or there are negative words exchanged (bad seeds planted).

Literally, the power of life or death for any relationship is in your mouth. You possess an incredible ability to give life or death, encouragement or discouragement, truth or deception, praise or criticism, hurt or help to those around you.

To understand this issue fully, you must first recognize how your own family history and the culture around you can shape the way you communicate. We live in a smart-aleck, sarcastic, and immoral culture. Words are thrown around as if they don't matter, and people are treated as though they had little worth. Just watch a little television and you'll get my point.

Also, if you are from a verbally abusive family or have lived in a negative verbal environment, you will have the tendency to follow that pattern of behavior. It is important to realize the unhealthy manner in which those around you communicate and to refuse to follow suit. If you will notice, you can see that those who are impure, ungodly, or negative in their speech do not have good relationships.

Words are like seeds. If you don't like the harvest in your marriage, there is good news: you can change seeds and the harvest will change. You have power. You aren't helpless and you aren't a victim. You have the power of death and life in your tongue. Unleash that power toward your spouse in a positive manner and you will see the truth of what the Bible says.

Talk It Out 💬
Ask each other these questions, and answer honestly (but kindly!).

+ **Do I communicate with you enough?**
+ **Do I communicate praise and appreciation to you enough?**
+ **Have I spoken negative or hurtful words that I need to apologize for?**

Walk It Out ☑
Write down several positive, affirming things you would like to say to your spouse. Putting them down on paper first helps you select just the right words. Exchange papers sometime before next week's devotional time.

Write It Out 📋

His

Hers

Relationship

Creating a culture of love

The Formula for Love

Love is patient, love is kind, and is not jealous; love does not brag and is not arrogant, does not act unbecomingly; it does not seek its own.
(1 Corinthians 13:4-5 NAS)

Did you know there are reasons we love the people we do? There are two things we all have in common about those we love. First, we admire something about the people we love. Second, they make us feel good about ourselves.

This formula for love never changes—it is always true. Even in our relationship with Christ, it's true.

For instance, I love Christ because I admire Him. There is no one I admire more. But admiration for His character and nature is not the only reason I love Him. I love Christ because of what He did for me on the cross, and what He does for me daily in my relationship with Him. He makes me feel valued, special, and secure. I love the way He makes me feel about me.

The truth is, you will never fall in love with a person who makes you feel bad about yourself.

Just think about the "puppy love" phase of your relationship. You were attracted to each other and couldn't wait to spend time together. The reason was twofold. You liked something about the other person, and you liked the way he or she made you feel about yourself.

Now let's talk about how a breakdown in a love relationship occurs. One of the most crucial roles you play in your husband's or wife's life is to be God's instrument in revealing to them that they are very important and special. When you are no longer feeding each other's self-esteem and regularly highlighting the things you admire about each other, the formula for love begins to break down.

The good news is, this situation is easily reversed. As you make it a point to look for and talk about the qualities you admire in each other, you will begin rebuilding each other's self-esteem. With a little bit of effort, you will be able to see immediate results. The way your husband or wife makes you feel will improve noticeably, and you'll discover that the formula for love is easier than you might have thought!

Talk It Out 💬

Try looking at your relationship from your spouse's perspective by asking yourself the question, "How healthy would my self-esteem be if I were married to me?" Share your thoughts and talk about ways to make improvements in this area. Take turns talking about the qualities you admire in each other.

Walk It Out ☑

One night this week, give each other a 10-minute (or longer) massage. While giving your spouse a massage, talk about the things you admire and appreciate most about him or her.

Write It Out 📄

His

....

....

....

....

....

....

....

Hers

....

....

....

....

....

....

....

The Difference Faith Makes

Now faith is the substance of things hoped for, the evidence of things not seen. (Hebrews 11:1)

Hebrews 11:6 says that it is impossible to please God without faith. Every good thing that God does in our lives is in response to our faith in Him and His Word. It pleases Him when we believe in His presence and His good intentions for us. In other words, faith works when we believe in the unseen presence of God and His unfailing love. Faith withers when we doubt that He is with us in an intimate manner or that He loves us as our Heavenly Father.

In marriage, faith must be exercised every day and in every area of life. Faith gets our eyes off of each other and the smaller issues and puts them on a big God. When we pray in faith, not only do we see God answer with miracles, but we also find a place of unity and peace in the midst of the worst storms in life.

Karen and I have learned that if we don't pray, we will worry and probably fight. Worse still, if we don't pray, we don't see God work as only He can. We have seen literally hundreds, if not thousands, of answers to prayer over the thirty+ years of our marriage. Faith in God is a bond between us that is stronger than any force that can come against us or try to tear us apart.

Faith becomes especially crucial when you see an area of weakness in your spouse. I verbally abused and dominated Karen for the first several years of our marriage because I wanted her to change. I thought the force of my words and personality could do it. It didn't. The only thing it did was to ruin our marriage and almost cause a divorce.

Karen didn't change until I put faith in God, did what the Bible said, and trusted God for the results. I remember when I learned to say something once to Karen in a loving manner and then to pray for God to enforce it. The results were amazing!

God cares about every detail of your life, and He is ready to act on your behalf when you put faith in Him. As you pray and believe, God will come through for you.

Talk It Out 🗩

Ask yourself these two important questions: Do you have faith in God? And do you exercise faith related to your marriage? Talk about the areas of your marriage that you're ready to stop worrying or fighting about and start trusting in God. Pray together and begin to believe God to see a change.

Walk It Out ☑

Pick out a favorite Bible verse this week, write it down and share it with your spouse. Make it a special reminder to both of you that God is working in your marriage and that you can trust Him with any situation, big or small.

Write It Out 📝

His

Hers

Getting Real About Anger

Be angry, and do not sin; do not let the sun go down on your wrath, nor give place to the devil. (Ephesians 4:26-27)

Every marriage has problems, even good marriages. The difference between a good and a bad marriage is simply the ability to work through problems. The good news is that every person can learn the skills of successful conflict resolution. Regardless of the mistakes you may have made in the past, you can turn your marriage and life around by learning these skills. And these skills work in more than just marriage; they help you in every relationship.

One of the first principles of conflict resolution is how to deal with anger. In Ephesians 4:26, the first thing that the Apostle Paul tells us about dealing with anger is that we must acknowledge it. He says, "Be angry..." Denying anger doesn't make it go away; instead, it makes it build up until it explodes in a destructive and unmanageable manner.

Anger isn't necessarily good or bad; it's just real. As human beings, we get angry. Sometimes it is because we've been genuinely violated. In other cases, it's because we're immature or have unrealistic expectations or are selfish. When I'm angry and need to get it out, I'm not claiming that I'm right; I'm just angry.

When Karen and I got married, we didn't know how to deal with anger. We both stuffed a lot of it inside and about every three months we would have an explosive fight. Sometimes our fights were about the dumbest little things, but those dumb little things were just the spark that caused the stored up anger inside of us to explode.

Jimmy Evans

Write It Out 📄
Week 27

His

_____

_____

_____

_____

_____

_____

_____

Hers

_____

_____

_____

_____

_____

_____

_____

Man of the House

For you, dear friends, have been called to live in freedom—not freedom to satisfy your sinful nature, but freedom to serve one another in love. (Gal. 5:13 NLT)

Many police cars have this slogan on the side: "To protect and to serve." The authority of a husband as the head of his home exists for the same two purposes. Righteous authority can only be used in this manner. Any other use of authority is abusive and self-serving.

The misuse of authority has led many women to flinch when the word *submission* is brought up. Today's women often view submission to men as an outdated and humiliating concept. Much of this response is due to the failure of men to be Christlike leaders in their homes.

Let's go back to the two purposes of authority. One of the reasons God gives men the position as head of the home is to protect his wife. Let me give you an example of this in my own marriage. First of all, Karen is my equal. My authority as her husband isn't about domination or superiority. It's about protection.

Every good marriage thrives on cooperation and respect. So when do I use authority? I use it when I see Karen doing something that would put her at risk. An example is her back. She had an injury about fifteen years ago that led to a surgery. The only time you will ever see me being bossy with Karen is when I see her about to lift something that would damage her back. Men should protect their wives. The Bible uses the word *cherish* to describe how husbands should love their wives. It means to protect from all harm.

The other purpose of authority is to serve. Jesus was a servant leader and taught us to be the same. Men should be the servant leaders of their homes. This means two things. First of all it means that he is the loving initiator of the well-being of the home—respecting his wife as his equal. Rather than being passive or dominant, a servant leader initiates discussions and actions related to such things as children, finances, spirituality, and romance as he invites the advice and influence of his wife.

The second thing that a servant leader does is use his position to bring others to their highest potential. The Bible says a man should nourish his wife. The word *nourish* in that text means to "feed to maturity." A good husband is God's partner to bring his wife to the full purpose God created her for— which is always great. When a wife knows that her husband is her biggest fan and is there to promote and protect her, she's in heaven.

Talk It Out 💬
Wives, tell your husband about a time that you appreciated his role in protecting and serving you. Tell him how it made you feel and why it's important to you. As a couple, talk about ways you can deepen your sense of cooperation in your marriage.

Walk It Out ☑
Look at some pictures from early in your marriage or when you were dating. Talk about some of your favorite memories.

Write It Out 📋
Week 28

His

_____

_____

_____

_____

_____

_____

Hers

_____

_____

_____

_____

_____

_____

A Woman's Place

The wisdom that is from above is first pure, then peaceable, gentle, willing to yield, full of mercy and good fruits, without partiality and without hypocrisy. (James 3:17)

This week I want to talk about the importance of men receiving influence from their wives. Women are more naturally open to receiving input from their husbands and sharing when it comes to relationships. However, men can view receiving input and influence from their wives as being weak.

It is common for men to fear being henpecked or controlled by their wives. In spite of the progress that has been made in the arena of women's rights, male chauvinism is alive and well. But beyond the issue of male chauvinism, there is a natural pride in just about every man that makes him highly sensitive to the issue of honor and esteem.

This is why men don't stop and ask for directions when they are lost. It is also the reason they can be resistant to receiving advice and input from their wives. For all of the men reading this, I want you to know that it is very important for you to learn to receive input from your wife and to let her know that you value her ideas and feelings. Your need for esteem is important. But your wife's need to feel valued in the relationship is of equal importance.

When Karen and I first got married, I was chauvinistic and very insecure. When Karen shared with me, I would roll my eyes, make sarcastic comments and let her know in no uncertain terms that I didn't value her input. I'm a different man today. I deeply value Karen's input; she is God's gift to me. In every area of our marriage and my personal life, she has enriched me. She helps put me in touch with feelings I am not sensitive to without her. She helps me make better decisions because she has a unique perspective that broadens my viewpoint.

Karen has such incredible wisdom. I have learned to listen to her and value her ideas and feelings. It really makes a woman feel special and secure in a marriage when she knows her input is received. Few things hurt a woman more than to be rejected and devalued by her husband as she tries to share her viewpoints.

Women are a gift from God. Society is greatly benefited by the influence women bring to men. Without them, men are much less productive and much more dangerous to themselves and others. The more men understand how much they need women and value their input, the better they are.

Talk It Out 💬
Husbands, let your wife know that you are thankful for her. Communicate to her how much you appreciate her ideas and feelings. Ask her for input in a decision or issue you are dealing with right now, and show her how much you value that input.

Walk It Out ☑
Do something special this week to let your spouse know how much you love him or her. Send her flowers or buy him that cd he's been wanting. Include a love note with your gift.

Jimmy Evans

Write It Out 📄
Week 29

His

_____

_____

_____

_____

_____

_____

_____

_____

Hers

_____

_____

_____

_____

_____

_____

_____

_____

Sensitive Issues

So as those who have been chosen of God, holy and beloved, put on a heart of compassion, kindness, humility, gentleness and patience. (Col. 3:12 nas)

Humans are tender creatures. All of us are. Even though many times we pretend things don't bother us, many things really do. I remember a situation that began with a phone call late one night from a frantic wife. She called us for help because she and her husband were having a terrible fight and he was packing to leave.

When we arrived at their home, it was chaotic. She was in the living room with the children. They were all very upset and crying. He was in the garage loading his car to leave. Karen tried to comfort her and I talked to him in the garage.

Here is the short version. The husband was the type of person who hid his personal pain beneath a tough exterior. The more hurt and afraid he felt, the more dominant and intimidating he acted. He'd found out weeks earlier that his wife had some physical problems that were pretty serious. He was concerned and told her to go to the doctor. She didn't. Every time he reminded her she would just brush him off.

On the night of the fight, he became very dominant and forceful with her about another issue. However, what was really bothering him was the thought that she might die. He cherished her and couldn't stand the thought that her medical problems might be terminal. His fears took over and emotions got out of control.

Jimmy Evans

As we sat with them and talked things out, she watched him sob uncontrollably as he talked about how much he loved her and how afraid he was something might happen to her. She admitted that the reason she didn't go to the doctor was because the possible cost. As you can see, both were bothered by something and both of their concerns were valid. However, because they didn't honestly discuss their feelings, the situation nearly ended in tragedy.

I've learned over the years that everything matters. Because of that, I am honest about my feelings and sensitive to Karen's. I realize that when I'm bothered by something Karen says or does, there is usually more to her behavior.

Rather than reacting to what she says, I've learned to pursue what is going on with her on a deeper level. On many occasions, this has kept me from reacting with rejection, withdrawal or verbal aggression. It has also caused me to deeply respect the sensitivity of Karen's heart and my own as well.

Talk It Out 💬
What underlying issues in your relationship are you reluctant to bring to the surface and talk about? This would be a good time to begin a conversation about sensitive issues that really matter and allow your spouse to see it from your perspective.

Walk It Out ☑
Call your spouse at an unexpected time this week, just to say, "I'm thinking of you."

Write It Out 📝
Week 30

His

Hers

Week 31

Worth the Effort

Husbands, love your wives, just as Christ also loved the church and gave Himself for it. (Ephesians 5:25)

I recently saw another report about how male sweat causes positive responses in women. The latest research was published by the University of California. In testing the effects of male sweat on women, they once again recorded positive hormonal changes for the majority of them who were exposed to its smell. This is significant.

First of all, those hormonal changes indicate sexual arousal. For any man who is looking for a way to rev up his wife's libido, this is it. This is really good news—but there is a twist involved. To produce sweat, you have to exert effort. Jumping in a sauna and collecting sweat in a jar that you put under your wife's nose probably won't produce the desired result.

The issue is how God has wired women to respond to a sacrificial, servant-hearted man. Besides the sweat research, studies have shown that wives find their husbands sexually attractive when they are doing housework. Men really need to understand the truth of this. Whereas males are sexually wired to respond to visual stimuli, women respond more to emotional stimuli. Specifically, they are attracted to men who serve them and help around the house.

Another important element of the sweat research has to do with the calming influence male sweat has on women. A study that was conducted at the University of Pennsylvania found that male sweat causes women to relax and feel happy.

To look at the other side of this, without sweat, women tend to be more tense and less happy. I know a lot of men who wonder why their wives are so uptight and hormonal (in the negative sense). In many cases, it just goes back to the fact that they feel as though they are not being supported and served by their husbands. In other words, they just need to get a whiff of a little sweat around the house to calm down and get into a better mood.

When Karen and I first got married, I wanted her to honor me and respond to me sexually. I tried everything I knew to get the results I wanted. However, since I was very selfish at the time, serving Karen and helping around the house wasn't something I tried very often.

Over the years as I have matured and grown as a husband, I have noticed that Karen is very uncomplicated. The more she feels as though I care and am there to support her, the more naturally honoring and sexually responsive she is. Even if I don't break a sweat, her response is consistent.

Talk It Out 💬
What does the "sweat meter" at your house reveal? Talk about the times you have noticed this principle at work in your marriage. Be open and honest about ways to improve in this area.

Walk It Out ☑
Husbands, do a specific chore for your wife this week. It could be running an errand, shopping for groceries, or doing something around the house. (Based on the research referenced above, housework might be a good choice!).

Write It Out 📄
Week 31

His

_____

_____

_____

_____

_____

_____

_____

Hers

_____

_____

_____

_____

_____

_____

_____

Feast or Famine?

The generous will prosper; those who refresh others will themselves be refreshed. (Proverbs 11:25 NLT)

There is a story I heard years ago about the difference between heaven and hell. It isn't a biblically accurate story, but that's not the point. It is accurate related to human behavior and how our attitudes affect our happiness in life and in marriage. Here it is:

In heaven and in hell, people are seated around a banquet table and before them is a great feast. There is a strange dilemma, however, about the way they must eat. Every person has eating utensils strapped to their hands that they cannot take off. Also, the utensils are too long for them to feed themselves. There is no way they could scoop food and return it to their own mouths.

In heaven, the people easily find the solution. With joy, they simply feed each other and have a great time of fellowship as they serve one another and enjoy the feast that heaven offers. Hell is much different. The people in hell are so selfish that they would rather starve to death than help someone else. Therefore, even though they have the same food available, they never experience it because they refuse to serve each other.

Like I said before, it isn't an accurate account of what the Bible says; however, it is a very accurate picture of the difference between bad and good marriages. The primary difference in many cases between success or failure in marriage is simply whether you are motivated by selfishness or a servant attitude.

Just like in the story, a banquet is set before us in marriage. Both of us bring to the relationship amazing giftings, abilities, and personality that can nourish and bless our spouses. However, they can only be experienced if we focus on each other and are willing to serve and give.

I remember back to the "hell" days in our marriage when I was too selfish to meet Karen's needs or focus on her. We lived in an emotional wilderness where both of us were miserable. I also remember when our season in hell ended and the "heaven" years began approximately thirty years ago. I saw the light and repented for my selfishness. Since then Karen and I have been committed to serving each other and meeting each other's needs.

I like the story of heaven and hell. It's a good reminder to all of us not to be selfish. Just remember, your marriage is full of every blessing you can ever hope for, but it can only be released as you are willing to serve your spouse.

Talk It Out 💬
What are some of the giftings and abilities that each of you bring into the marriage relationship? Write down the positive qualities you see in your spouse, and compare your lists. Then talk about ways you can use those giftings to meet each other's needs.

Walk It Out ☑
Prepare a food item that your spouse really likes, and take turns serving the food to each other. It could be something as simple as microwave popcorn or it could be a full-course meal—whatever you choose. Use this as an opportunity to demonstrate your desire to serve each other.

Write It Out 📓

His

Hers

Imagination

Desiring the best for your marriage

Romance for Two

Now abide faith, hope, love, these three; but the greatest of these is love. (1 Corinthians 13:13)

About ten years ago my uncle Charles died. He was a good man and had a happy marriage of forty years to my aunt Peggy. As I was preparing to do his eulogy at the funeral, my aunt told me that he wrote her a new poem every day before he went to work and left it on the kitchen table. Wow! Obviously, he understood the importance of keeping their romance alive on a daily basis.

One of the biggest misconceptions in marriage is that romance can be infrequent and a marriage will still stay strong. No relationship can be maintained solely through the right chemistry or the idea of being "soul mates." A strong relationship is the product of developing the right relational habits and exercising important skills that help build and maintain a strong marriage.

So let's talk about what romance is and what it isn't. When you are romantic, you communicate a unique value to your spouse. It's an action that says, "You are on my heart and I care about our relationship." Romance means meeting an unspoken need or desire. If your spouse has to keep reminding you to do something special, it takes the romance out of the gesture. It is only romantic if you take the *initiative* to do something that your spouse will enjoy.

Also, a romantic gesture must be in a "language" your spouse understands. This is where many men and women

Jimmy Evans

make mistakes. Romance for a woman means physical affection without sex. It also means verbal affection—a lot of meaningful conversation. Meeting her relational needs in a patient and caring manner is very romantic to a woman. Sex is not the primary issue for her. When she is sexual, it is in response to her emotional needs being met.

Romance means something very different for a man. He doesn't need candlelight dinners and long walks to be romanced. There are two essentials elements involved in romance for him: honor and sex. A naked cheerleader is a perfect solution for his romantic needs!

The important thing is to communicate value and respect to your partner while demonstrating a servant's spirit. The more you romance your spouse, the more passionate and healthy your marriage will become.

Talk It Out 💬
Describe to each other what your definition of romance is. Remember, there are no right or wrong answers; it's simply your perspective of what makes you feel special and loved.

Walk It Out ☑
Sometime this week, do one of the things that your spouse identified as a gesture that would be especially romantic to him or her. Make sure it's something that speaks your spouse's romance language, not yours.

Write It Out 📄

His

_____

_____

_____

_____

_____

_____

_____

Hers

_____

_____

_____

_____

_____

_____

_____

Building Trust

Who can find a virtuous wife? For her worth is far above rubies. The heart of her husband safely trusts her; so he will have no lack of gain. She does him good and not evil all the days of her life. (Proverbs 31:10-12)

Trust is an essential element of intimacy and goodwill in marriage. The more you trust your spouse, the more you can relax when you're together and open your hearts to each other. This is what makes a "comfortable" relationship. That doesn't mean comfortable in the bad sense, where you are lazy and take each other for granted. This is comfortable in the best sense of the word.

The rewards of trust are immense. An example is sexual fulfillment. Nationwide polls prove that the best sex isn't experienced by swinging singles. It is experienced mostly by married, monogamous, religious people.

I believe the reason for this is simple. Even though singles in a casual relationship may share a sexual encounter, the relationship remains superficial and performance-oriented. Rejection is frequent and trust is low, which contributes to decreased sexual gratification. However, in a committed relationship, trust is much higher and sex is better.

Another reward is in the area of communication. When you trust each other, it is easy to share your thoughts without fear and to resolve issues. You communicate on a much deeper level, which brings a sense of intimate friendship.

such things as perfect friends, even if they are very godly people you meet in church. However, perfection isn't the issue. The issue is that you have a support group around you encouraging you to do the right thing as you also encourage them.

The last thing you need when you are going through tough times in marriage is someone encouraging you to do the wrong thing. You need wise counsel and prayer from a person of faith and character. Karen and I are blessed with good, godly friends. They have stood with each other through many years of mountaintops and valleys of life.

Don't be deceived; bad company will corrupt your morals and your marriage. Break off unhealthy relationships and work to create healthy ones. The best place I know of to meet good friends is in a Bible-based church. The people there aren't perfect any more than you are, but they are people who share your values and will be an essential support base for a successful marriage.

Talk It Out 🗩

Honestly evaluate your friendships and speak up about any concerns you have. If you identify that some of your friendships aren't healthy for your marriage, make a commitment to seek out the kind of friends who share your values.

Walk It Out ☑

Invite another couple over for dinner or go out to a movie together. Spend time cultivating friendships that have a positive effect on your marriage.

Write It Out 📝

His

Hers

Mind Your Manners

A word fitly spoken is like apples of gold in settings of silver. (Proverbs 25:11)

Have you ever wondered why manners are so important?

Well, for one thing, *manners preserve relationships*. That's right. When manners are lacking, people may feel violated and relationships can be threatened.

This is especially true in a marriage relationship. In fact, when the honeymoon phase of a marriage comes to a close, emotions may begin to deteriorate if a couple fails to display basic manners toward one another.

Let me give you several examples. When two people begin dating, they typically display very good manners, right? They show appreciation by saying "thank you"; they show consideration by being sensitive and courteous to each other; the man shows care for the woman by opening doors for her; and so on.

As the relationship progresses, it is often typical for a husband and wife to begin to take each other for granted and stop exercising good manners. He or she may fail to show appreciation by saying "thank you"; they are not as sensitive or courteous to one another; a husband may stop opening doors for his wife; and so on.

Manners, however, are very important —they are indicators of the kind of people we are. The presence of manners means that you are a giver. The lack of manners means that you are a taker. The presence of manners means that you are not self-centered. The absence of manners means you are selfish. The presence of manners means that you value others. The absence of manners means that you don't.

Remember, manners preserve relationships. They preserve a marriage and promote goodwill between a husband and wife.

God's design is for marriage to get progressively *better* every year. It is never His intention for a marriage to experience an emotional slump for any significant period of time. A lack of passion and goodwill between a husband and wife indicates something is missing in the relationship—primarily good manners.

Talk It Out 🗩

How are your manners? Do you treat your spouse the way you did when you first met? Do you treat strangers better than your spouse? An honest assessment of your marriage manners can help you discover a lot about yourself and the overall health of your marriage relationship.

Walk It Out ☑

Think about ways you may have gotten too comfortable and relaxed around each other. Put forth a little effort to change one thing this week—for example, dressing up and looking nice for each other, actively listening when your spouse is talking, etc.

Write It Out 📄

His

Hers

Keeping Out Intrusions

And the peace of God, which surpasses all understanding, will guard your hearts and minds through Christ Jesus. (Philippians 4:7)

I was at a hotel recently, and while I was checking in at the reception desk, the young lady who was helping me regularly answered the telephone and broke away from helping me to solve someone else's problems. I have to admit, that is one of my pet peeves.

My belief is that the person who is standing before you in the flesh should take priority over someone who is calling on the phone. But in most cases—in hotels and other businesses—it is the opposite.

Likewise, I know of many people who are completely frustrated by the constant intrusion of other people into their spouse's lives through technology. It has become a major issue in our world today. Whether it is a cell phone call, text message, email, MySpace page hit or something else, we are being bombarded by outsiders trying to get into our lives. Just like my experience in the hotel, in many cases, the one we are with is put on hold for the one calling in.

The result in many marriages is frustration and feelings of rejection. Many spouses feel as if there is virtually no time, no place, and no person that is protected from these intrusions.

To address this growing problem, we need to first of all go back to the issue of good manners. It is simply bad manners to allow someone to intrude upon our conversations and important time together.

Make technology your servant and not your master. You need to remind yourself that you can survive without being constantly connected to everyone else at all times. In fact, you must have times when you disconnect and keep others away. Call it a "technology time out" or "electronic Sabbath." Just do it.

I am very connected electronically and use a cell phone and email regularly throughout the day, but not at night and not when I'm spending important time with Karen. When we are together, we will many times not answer phone calls out of respect for each other. We realize the fact that we must manage the blessing of technology or it can become a curse.

Talk It Out 💬

Does your spouse know that he or she is a priority and won't be at the mercy of the next phone call, text message, or email? Talk about ways to prioritize and show honor to each other, and about how to keep electronic intrusions from damaging your relationship.

Walk It Out ☑

Spend time together in the evenings without any intrusions or distractions—no TV, cell phones, computer, etc. Use this time for uninterrupted conversation, or just snuggle on the couch and enjoy each other's company.

Write It Out 📝

His

Hers

Jimmy Evans

A Fruitful Endeavor

Do not be deceived, God is not mocked; for whatever a man sows, that he will also reap. (Galatians 6:7)

One of the most important principles in Scripture is that of sowing and reaping. From the beginning of Creation until now, the law of seedtime and harvest has been in operation, affecting every aspect of our life here on earth. For instance, in the agricultural world, in the animal kingdom, and even in human reproduction, we easily can understand how a seed implanted will produce a harvest. But do you realize the principle of sowing and reaping is always in progress in your marriage as well?

Your mouth is a seed warehouse. Words are some of the most powerful seeds you sow; they are so powerful they can have a disproportionate effect on your marriage. By that I mean your words have the ability to affect your spouse and marriage more than almost anything else (see Proverbs 18:20-21; James 3:2-6).

In addition to the words you speak, your actions and attitudes are also seeds that are being sown into the lives of those around you. And they will produce a harvest, whether good or bad. Inconsequential behavior simply does not exist.

Here is how the Apostle Paul puts it: *For he who sows to his flesh will of the flesh reap corruption, but he who sows to the Spirit will of the Spirit reap everlasting life. And let us not grow weary while doing good, for in due season we shall reap if we do not lose heart. Therefore, as we have opportunity, let us do*

good to all, especially to those who are of the household of faith.
(Galatians 6:8-10)

When you notice attitudes, words, or behaviors in your spouse that make you unhappy, you need to consider the fact that to some degree you may be responsible for the negative behavior. It's possible that you are reaping the results of what you have sown into your husband's or wife's life.

Of course, the same law of sowing and reaping applies when good seeds are sown. You can kill off a bad crop by simply repenting before God and your spouse for your negative words and actions. Then begin planting a new crop by carefully and purposefully sowing good seed in your marriage and all areas of your life. Your harvest then will be a good one! It may not be an instant harvest, but it is a guaranteed one.

Talk It Out ⌨

What kind of seeds are you sowing into your marriage? Repent to each other for any negative words or behavior, and talk about specific ways to change the negatives into positives.

Walk It Out ☑

Speak out loud what the Bible says about your spouse and your marriage. Look up verses that tell of God's blessings, and speak God's Word over your situation. That seed has the power of God to make a profound impact in every area of your relationship.

Write It Out 📝
Week 48

His

Hers

Precision Required

Whoever hears these sayings of Mine, and does them, I will liken him to a wise man who built his house on the rock: and the rain descended, the floods came, and the winds blew and beat on that house; and it did not fall, for it was founded on the rock. (Matthew 7:24-25)

In almost every realm of life, success depends on precision. The examples are almost endless. Tiger Woods must hit the ball in a precise position and putt it exactly in the hole. He must do this for eighteen holes each day and for four days in a row to win a golf tournament.

Those who assemble airplanes must build them to exact specifications for safety reasons. Those who manufacture medications, especially those to treat serious illnesses, must make them to conform to the most precise mixture of ingredients and dosages. The list goes on and on as to the areas of life that must be precise for success.

Marriage is the same. It must be conducted according to God's specific plan if it is going to work. I'm saying this for two reasons. First, I'm simply reminding you that God created man and marriage, and He is the only person who truly understands how we operate.

The Word of God is the instruction book that tells how you are designed to operate. In His mercy, God has given detailed instructions showing you how to love each other and how to build a life and marriage that will stand every test. In the

Scripture above, Jesus promises that if you will obey His words, no force on earth will be able to cause you to fail.

The second reason I am addressing this issue is because of how common it is for people to try to make their marriages and relationships work on their own terms. This is true of many married couples who ignore God's Word and try to impose their own opinions on each other to fix their problems or to alleviate frustrations.

World history and recent American history are replete with examples of how marriage is a miserable failure when you don't follow God's instructions. Just like most other areas of life, marriage requires precision. Thank God that He has given you every answer needed for success.

Next time you're flying on an airplane, be thankful that those who put it together were precise. It's what makes your flight safe and pleasant. It's the same for marriage. Buckle up, get your Bible out and enjoy a safe and pleasant life.

Talk It Out 💬
Talk about everyday ways that precision is important in your life—for example, measuring ingredients for a recipe, balancing your checkbook, following safety procedures at work, etc. Then discuss how that principle carries over into your marriage. In what areas could you apply God's Word more precisely to ensure success?

Walk It Out ☑
Watch a favorite movie together one night this week. Pop some popcorn or fix a snack you both like; then cuddle up on the couch and enjoy!

Write It Out 📝

His

Hers

Week 50

Dreaming Big

Now this is the confidence that we have in Him, that if we ask anything according to His will, He hears us. And if we know that He hears us, whatever we ask, we know that we have the petitions that we have asked of Him. (1 John 5:14-15)

Research proves that the best marriages are those with high goals. It's important that you set goals for your marriage and keep your expectations high. However, high goals must also be accompanied by realistic expectations.

There are two extremes that cause a lot of marriage problems. On the one hand, it is common to see couples who have very high expectations for their marriages but also have a fairy tale mentality that everything good is just going to fall into their proverbial laps. Unrealistic expectations set them up for heartache and disappointment.

On the other extreme are the couples who don't want to be disappointed so they keep their expectations low. Sometimes these couples are cynical because of failed marriages in their past or chronic problems in their present marriage.

Finding balance is the key to success. You must set goals and have dreams for your marriage. You must also realize that there will be challenges along the way and enemies you must face and overcome. By the way, the journey toward the dream is as important as the dream itself. It is on the journey that you learn to depend on each other, trust in each other, pray together and ultimately become close friends and intimate lovers.

Another important issue in setting high goals is to learn to establish practical disciplines in your relationship that move you toward your goals. They need to be things your regular schedule can accommodate and things you'll stick with. Here are a few practical suggestions:

+ Have a date night every week. Do something special and work hard on that night to keep your romance alive.
+ Commit to having a vision retreat this year (which I talked about in week 44, A Common Vision).
+ Be creative and energetic in meeting each other's needs.
+ Brush up on your manners. Recommit to appreciating each other and honoring each other.
+ Go to at least one marriage seminar this year, and read at least one marriage book together.

Be inspired to set some new goals and keep dreaming big dreams for your marriage. God created you for greatness.

Talk It Out 💬

What goals have you set for your marriage? Do you have realistic expectations of how to attain them? Write down your common goals and pray together, asking God to help you realize your dreams.

Walk It Out ☑

Make this week's date night specifically for her. Husbands, let your wife choose what you will do on your date, and put extra effort into making it special for her!

Jimmy Evans

Write It Out 📓

His

Hers

Making Dreams Come True

The hopes of the godly result in happiness, but the expectations of the wicked come to nothing. (Proverbs 10:28 NLT)

Research has shown that many of the more serious fights in marriage occur on a dream level. What this means is that in your heart you entertain certain deeply embedded desires and dreams. Many of them go back for many years, even into your childhood. Also, many of them are so deeply entrenched in your psyche that you don't think of them on a conscious level.

For example, it is common for a woman to have the dream of living in a house with a white picket fence. Women also commonly dream of having a loving husband who is a present partner with them in raising a family.

It is common for men to dream of having a wife who adores them and thinks they hung the moon. Men often dream of having a wife who takes care of the house well and prepares good meals for them.

With your dreams deeply lodged within your heart, you embark upon marriage. Your hopes run high when you are dating and even during the honeymoon phase of marriage. The problems surface when you begin to violate each other's dreams.

For example, when a man begins to work late or stay out with his friends too often, he is violating his wife in obvious ways. However, what isn't so obvious is the fact that his insensitive behavior is actually ruining her chances of living out her dream.

On the other side, when he comes home and finds her angry and accusatory, his dream is also broken. It only makes matters worse if other areas of her behavior don't line up with what he has hoped for.

It is important for you to realize that everyone has dreams. It helps when you are able to bring those desires out in the open and talk about them together as a couple. What helps even more is a commitment to be each other's "dream makers" and not "dream breakers."

I encourage you to really think about this. Do you know what each other's dreams are? Have you made an effort to show you really care? Have you ever committed to make the other person's dreams come true? When you begin to make the necessary changes to stop violating each other's dreams, you've taken the first steps to making your marriage a dream come true.

Talk It Out 💬
Spend a few minutes separately thinking about your deepest dreams and desires for your marriage. Then come together and share those with each other. Talk about ways you can become each other's "dream makers."

Walk It Out ☑
This week, make your date night "his" night. Wives, take this chance to make your husband's dreams come true by focusing your attention and adoration on him.

Write It Out 📓

His

Hers

The Fork in the Road

I will instruct you and teach you in the way you should go; I will guide you with My eye. (Psalm 32:8)

The famous baseball player Yogi Berra has a way with words. Of his many famous quotes, this is one of my favorites: "When you come to the fork in the road, take it." He said it originally when giving someone directions to his home, because either way you turned at the fork, right or left, it still led to his house. Don't you wish it was that way in life?

The truth is, you will come to critical times in your life when you must make decisions as to which way you will turn. Will you forgive or hold a grudge? Will you stay and work things out or run from your problems? Will you withdraw from your spouse when he or she offends you and go elsewhere to get your needs met, or will you pursue your spouse and fight for your marriage?

In life, there are many proverbial "forks in the road." What you do at these times forms your character and forges your destiny. I recently met with a person who is bankrupt and has been divorced multiple times. He lamented to me that he had made every wrong choice at crucial times and wished he could go back and do it all over again.

Every marriage has problems and requires hard work and sacrifice for success. When you get to the difficult times in your life and marriage, you must forgive, commit and give of yourself in spite of your negative emotions. There will always be a little voice inside of you trying to convince you to take "the easy way"—the alternate road that looks so much more pleasing.

Also, at these times there are often supporters of that other path cheering you on and assuring you that you are justified in following your feelings. They want you to believe that the answer to all of your problems lies in the choice to do what God's Word says is wrong, but what the majority of people say is right.

As you conclude this 52-week devotional study, I want to leave you with two thoughts: first, the easy way is never easy. It is brutal. The pretty side of the fork in the road that is lined with flowers and goes downhill actually has many sharp turns with steep cliffs you can't see.

Second, the right way is the easiest way to live. Even though that side of the fork looks steep and rocky at first, it actually becomes a better road with every step you take. Also, as you climb higher and higher, the scenery becomes breathtaking as you see God's promises for your life, marriage, and family come true.

Talk It Out 🗨

What advice have you been given about your marriage that you knew was contrary to God's Word? And what voices have you had to choose to ignore in order to keep on the right path? Express to each other your commitment to continue on the road to building a healthy and fulfilling marriage.

Walk It Out ☑

Get together with another couple and share with them what this 52-week devotional experience has meant in your lives. Encourage them to begin the journey together!

Write It Out 📝

Week 52

His

Hers

Appendix

Appendix

In week 2, I talked about the importance of having a personal relationship with Jesus. You may be unsure of whether you have this kind of relationship, or you may realize you need one and want to know how. To help you, here are some basic truths:

1. God loves you personally. He created you in your mother's womb and He has a purpose for your life.

2. We are all sinners in God's sight. We could never be good enough on our own to earn our way to heaven.

3. Jesus paid the penalty for our sins through His death on the cross, and He conquered death when He was resurrected from the dead.

4. Forgiveness is available to anyone who repents of sin and invites Jesus to be Lord of their life.

According to Romans 10:9, here are the requirements for salvation: "If you confess with your mouth the Lord Jesus and believe in your heart that God has raised Him from the dead, you will be saved."